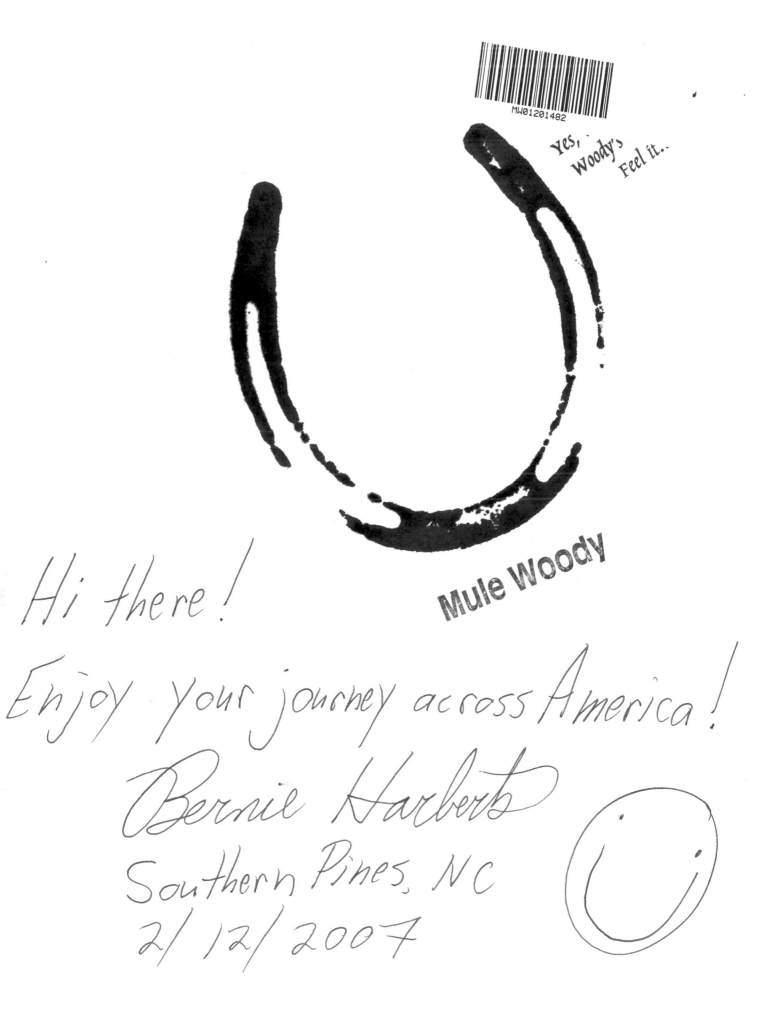

Yes, Woody's Feel it..

Mule Woody

Hi there!
Enjoy your journey across America!
Bernie Harberts
Southern Pines, NC
2/12/2007

RiverEarth Publishing
Post Office Box 245
Southern Pines, NC 28388 USA
info@riverearth.com; http://RiverEarth.com

Illustrations by Danila Devins and book layout by Elizabeth Phelps.

ISBN 10: 0-9787722-9-6
ISBN 13: 978-0-9787722-9-1

First Edition 2006
Second Edition 2006

Woody and Maggie Walk Across America

by Bernie Harberts

To Laura and Alvin, who got me seeing sky worms and swirly holes.

One day I decided to walk across America from North
Carolina to California — just to see what it was like.
I invited my friends to join me. But they were all too busy.

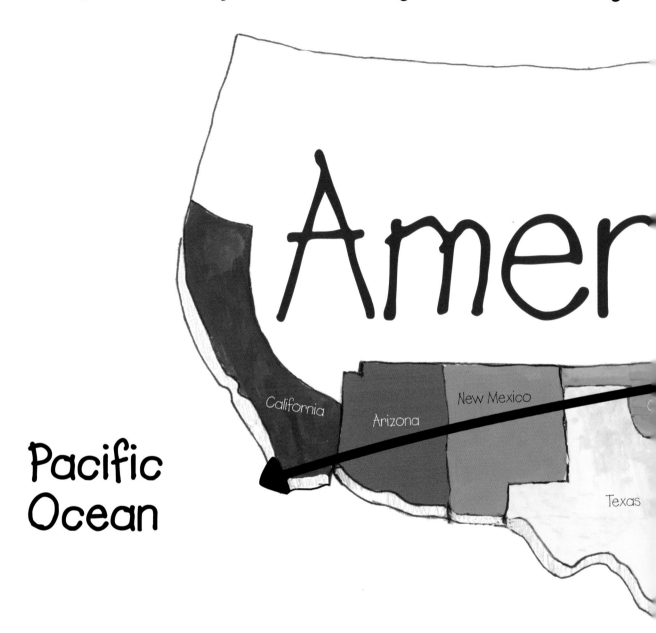

Pacific
Ocean

So I asked Woody and Maggie to come along.
Woody is *my mule* and Maggie is *my pony.*

"Come on," I said, "let's go to the Atlantic Ocean and fill this Mason jar with sea water. Then we'll walk across America. When we get to California, we'll pour it into the Pacific Ocean."

When I reached the Atlantic Ocean, Woody panicked, and I could barely fill *my* jar.

They looked at me funny, and I wondered what they were thinking. I also wondered what they were seeing. But they agreed to come along. So for the rest of our trip across America, I'll let Woody and Maggie tell you what they saw.

When I'm speaking, you'll see my picture next to my words. Like this:

When Woody and Maggie are speaking, you'll see their faces next to what they're saying. Like this:

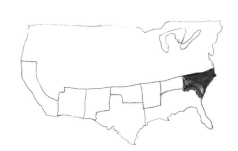

In North Carolina, fishermen use boats called trawlers to catch fish in big nets. They lower the nets into the water, and, after a while, they pull them up to see what they've caught. They're happy when they catch flounder, croaker, and trout and mad when they catch old tires and rusty anchors. They put the fish in big coolers and the anchors in their front yards.

The fish bird lives on the North Carolina coast. It's so big it can carry two men on its back but it can't fly because its wings are too weak. Every morning, it carries the men out on the ocean where they dip the bird's wings into the water. When the feathers touch the sea, they get longer and longer and fish get tangled in them. When the bird's wings are full of fish, the men pull them up and feed them to the bird. But no matter how many fish they feed it, the fish bird's wings never get strong enough to fly.

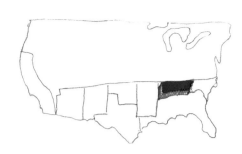

Tennessee is full of rivers. We could wade across the small ones. But to get across the big ones, like the Ocoee, we used bridges. On some bridges, there was too much traffic so I used a payphone to call the police for help. They would send out a squad car to escort us across. When the policeman turned on his red and blue lights, the traffic stopped. Then, while the cars waited, I rode Woody and Maggie across the bridge.

When Bernie has to cross a big river, he calls the river wizard for help. The wizard has one blue and one red eye. He flashes his eyes, and the cars freeze like ice, but we don't fall under his spell because we're not afraid. We just walk ahead of all those frozen cars. When we get to the other side of the river, the wizard stops blinking, the cars thaw out and then the wizard disappears.

When I needed groceries, I rode Woody and Maggie to a supermarket. I tied them to a light post and went inside to buy my rolled oats, split peas, olive oil and rice.

go shopping?

We live off hay and grain and Bernie eats lots of rice, but we've always wondered what cars eat. Now we know. They come to supermarkets where they gulp down things like dog food, watermelons, coffee makers and computers.

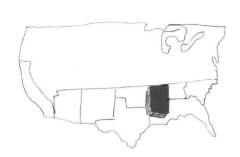

In Arkansas, many people have a "fraidy hole" in their back yard. It's just a little room buried in the ground that some people call a storm cellar. When the people hear a tornado might be coming, they jump into the fraidy hole because they know underground they'll be safe from the high winds.

The sky worm is a pesky critter that lives in the Arkansas sky. When it gets hungry, it jumps down from the clouds and eats barns and houses and trees. But it has really short teeth so it can't bite into the ground. That's why, when the people see a sky worm coming, they crawl into holes in the ground to live with the worms.

There's lots of oil buried under Oklahoma, and people use wells called pump jacks to suck it from the ground. The air around the wells smells smoky, like someone's burning an old tire. After the oil is pumped from the ground, it's sent to a refinery where it's turned into gasoline you can use in your car.

see in Oklahoma?

Oklahoma is covered in herds of really thirsty steel donkeys. They're snobs and won't talk to us because all they want to do is drink, drink, drink. All day they bob their heads up and down sucking car water from the ground through long straws. We know it's car water because, when the cars pass us, we can smell it on their breaths.

I slept inside a tipi instead of a house. In the evening, I pitched my tipi and put my wood stove together. I ran the smoke stack through the tipi roof, then built a fire in the stove so I could cook my supper.

you sleep?

Every night, Bernie opened one of his bags and shook out a giant mushroom. It was rotten, the stem was split and it had a bad temper. Then Bernie crawled inside, ate his dinner and stuck his feet through the hole in the stem. That made the mushroom really mad, and it blew steam out through its cap. But Bernie just ignored it.

In Texas, cattle ranchers use windmills to pump water from the ground for their cows. The water is stored in large containers called stock tanks. I often watered Woody and Maggie at windmills, and, after they finished drinking, I sometimes *jumped* in for a bath. The cows didn't seem to mind but I had to watch out for the frogs.

see in Texas?

Out on the Texas plains, they have enormous plants called wind flowers. Their heads spin in the breeze, and they squirt water from their belly buttons. They catch the water in their hands, and on hot days, Bernie lets us drink from their fingers.

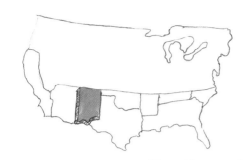

In New Mexico, ranchers use cattle guards where a fence crosses a road. A cattle guard is just a hole in the ground with steel pipes laid across it. Cows and horses are afraid to walk over the cattle guard because they're scared their feet will fall between the pipes. Next to each cattle guard, the ranchers install a gate. Whenever I came to a cattle guard, I just opened the gate and led Woody and Maggie through.

see in New Mexico?

New Mexico is full of swirly holes. A swirly hole is a deep hole in the ground with long teeth and an appetite for horse and cow legs. Next to each hole is a hand. Whenever Bernie had to pass a swirly hole, he walked over to the hand and shook it. The hand swung open and let us by. But it only opened for Bernie. It wouldn't open for us or the cows, no matter how hard we tried shaking it.

Danilo

 I often watered Woody and Maggie in rivers, lakes, windmills and sometimes swamps. But when I couldn't find water there, I asked people if I could get something to drink from their garden hose.

find water?

We like to drink from streams and ponds, but when they're scarce, Bernie looks for water snakes. They're green and sleep coiled up behind people's houses. When Bernie finds one, he puts its head over a bucket and twists its tail. That makes the snake really mad, and it spits the bucket full of water. Some days, when Bernie's hot and in a hurry, he just lets the water snake spit into his mouth. Yuck!

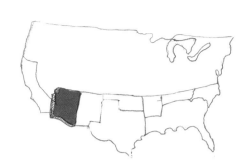

The saguaro cactus grows in the Arizona desert. A bird called the Gila woodpecker sometimes pecks a hole in the saguaro's trunk where it wants to build its nest. To keep from losing too much water through the injury, the cactus grows a protective layer around the hole. This is called a boot because that's what it looks like. When the saguaro dies and falls down, the boots pop out. They look like shoes scattered across the desert floor.

In Arizona, we came across families of naked green giants. Bandits had stolen their clothes and scattered their boots all over the desert. The giants were so embarrassed to be naked they didn't even gather up their shoes, so there was no way they could chase down the clothes thieves.

In California we crossed huge piles of sand called the Imperial Dunes. The sun was so bright, everyone we met wore sunglasses. As we traveled across the dunes, Woody and Maggie's feet sank deep into the powdery sand which made them very nervous.

see in California?

Everyone in California wore small black masks – the animals, too. We didn't see many animals, though, because during the day they hid in holes just below the surface of the sand. We sure wished they'd built stronger roofs because our feet kept falling through their ceilings. It scared us to step on a rattlesnake wearing its California mask.

After 13 months on the road. Woody, Maggie, and I arrived at the Pacific Ocean. I led them into the water.

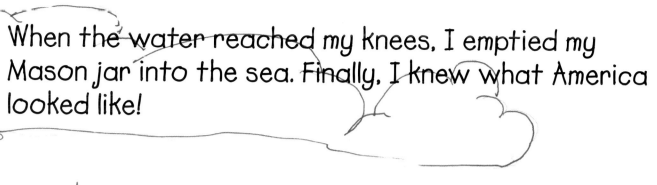

When the water reached my knees, I emptied my Mason jar into the sea. Finally, I knew what America looked like!

Now there was just one thing left to do. I had to get Woody and Maggie home.

At the end of my trip, my friends wanted to know if I was going to ride Woody and Maggie back to North Carolina. No, I told them, they had just walked over three thousand miles and deserved a rest. So I bought a truck and trailer and brought Woody and Maggie home in style.

get home?

When I got home, I turned Woody and Maggie back out in their pasture. Then I bought them the largest hay bale I could find.

They didn't come out from behind it for a week.

Congratulations! You've completed your journey across America with Woody, Maggie, and me.

Do you think you can find your way across the United States by yourself now?

Remember, you just have to get from one state to the next to make it to the other side.

On the next few pages, you will learn to identify each state so you can complete your journey.

If you get stuck just look back through the book for clues.

Good luck!

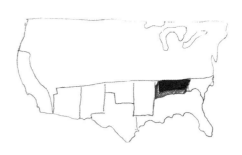

The state between the Atlantic Ocean and Tennessee is _____.

The state between North Carolina and Arkansas is _____.

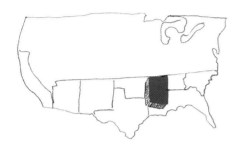

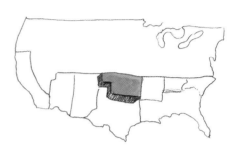

The state between Tennessee and Oklahoma is _____.

The state between Arkansas and New Mexico is _____.

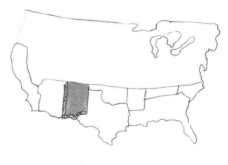

The state between Oklahoma and New Mexico is _____.

The state between Texas and Arizona is _____.

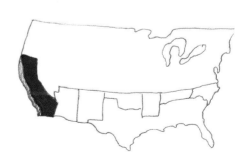

The state between New Mexico and California is _____.

The state between Arizona and the Pacific Ocean is _____.

Fisherman use trawlers in the state of _____.

Rivers with names like Ocoee flow in the state of _____.

Fraidy holes are buried in the state of _____.

Pump jacks pump oil in the state of _____.

Windmills pump water in the state of_____.

Cattle guards are found in the state of _____.

The saguaro cactus grows in the state of _____.

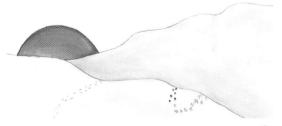

The Imperial Sand Dunes are found in the state of _____.

Fish birds carry men in the state of _____.

The river wizard freezes cars in the state of _____.

The sky worm eats trees in the state of _____.

Steel donkeys sip car water in the state of _____.

Wind flowers squirt water in the state of _____.

Swirly holes scare cows in the state of _____.

Naked green giants live in the state of _____.

Snakes wear black masks in the state of _____.

What really happened... by Bernie Harberts

Yes, "Woody and Maggie Walk Across America" is based on a true story.

In 2004/2005, Woody, Maggie and I really walked across America. We traveled alone, and we traveled slowly – on average, eight miles per day. We couldn't carry much gear, so instead we relied on the food, water, kindness and shelter of strangers.

This slow pace and human contact was the secret to discovering the America hidden from hurried travelers. At two miles-per-hour, we were able to absorb what set one state apart from the next.

I urge you to travel these pages at the same speed – at a pony's pace. Then take a closer look at the state you're in. Enjoy!

About the contributors

Woody was born on an Amish farm in Pennsylvania. Maggie is from West Virginia. She is the smallest pony to have walked from Southern Pines, NC to San Diego, California. Both still unseat Bernie regularly.

Bernie Harberts is a good writer, a fair horseman and a lousy judge of distance. He's sailed alone around the world and chronicles his travels at RiverEarth.com. When he's not living in a tipi, sailboat, mule wagon, or mushroom, he resides in North Carolina.

Danila Devins specializes in painting foxhunting scenes – with occasional forays into children's books. Danila, who was born in Florence, Italy and attended the Regio Istituto d'Arte, lives in Southern Pines, North Carolina.

RiverEarth.com

RiverEarth.com features the adventures of Bernie Harberts. Additional copies of "Woody and Maggie Walk Across America", along with Harberts' other work, are available at the website's online store.

Order Form

Online Orders: riverearth.com/store

Email Orders: store@riverearth.com

Postal Orders: RiverEarth, Bernie Harberts, PO Box 245, Southern Pines, NC 28388

Please send the following books or disks. I understand that I may return any of them for a full refund if I am not completely satisfied.

Title:	Price:
Title:	Price:
Title:	Price:
Shipping:	Price:
	Total:

Payment Method: Money order, credit card or personal check

Ship to:
Name:

Address:

City:

Telephone:

Email address:

Sales tax: Please include 7% for orders shipped to North Carolina addresses.

Shipping rates: Up to $25.00 purchase, shipping $3.95, $25.01 to $75.00, shipping $6.95, over $75.01, shipping $8.90.
International: $8.95 for first book or DVD, $4.95 for each additional item.